MY VERY
SPECIAL VISITOR

GLORIA HOUSE

PRESS

DEDICATION

I dedicate this book to my Lord and Savior Jesus Christ, who is my best friend and guide. Without You I can do nothing. My heart is overwhelmed with thankfulness for my very special visitor, the Holy Spirit, who has made this possible. My love for You grows and grows each day as I spend time in Your presence.

I am also thankful to my wonderful husband and three special sons whom God has given me, together with all my lovely grandchildren whom I treasure and love so very much. I'm also thankful for my beautiful mother, brothers, and sisters with whom God has blessed me. Thank you for all the good times and all the love I have experienced over the years. May God bless you abundantly and forever make His face to shine upon you.

I also appreciate my friends Maria, Marlene, Alicia and Joan for their support and advice during this project. It is clear God put you in my life for a reason. Together we continue our journey as we are led by the Holy Spirit.

CONTENTS

Chapter 1—Born to Live and Not Die 13

Chapter 2—A Very Special Visit by the
Holy Spirit 19

Chapter 3—My Need for a Miracle 24

Chapter 4—A Glimpse of Future Gifts into the
Prophetic 29

Chapter 5—A Divine Visit from Jesus 35

Chapter 6—After the Miracle 40

Chapter 7—Meeting the Love of my Life 46

Chapter 8—A Change from One Life to
Another 54

Chapter 9—The Amazing Birth of my
son Garrick 59

Chapter 10—A Divine Appointment with a
Salesman 65

Chapter 11—A Vacation where God's Glory is
Made Known 72

Chapter 12—Our Lives Take a Major Turn 79

Chapter 13—The Change That Happened on
New Year's Eve. 89

Chapter 14—Hearing from Heaven 96

Chapter 15—The Move to Florida that Changed
our Lives Forever 100

Chapter 16—Angel Visitation. 103

Chapter 17—The Gift from my Creator 111

Chapter 18—Release them to Fly. 121

FORWARD

J am deeply honored that I was asked to write the forward to this book. It has been greatly anticipated, and it is finally here.

The writer of this book, my wife Gloria, has fought long and hard for this book to take form. I pray that it blesses many as they read it, as I know it will.

The integrity and love for both God and people that you will find in these pages is just the tip of the iceberg. From a child of seven years to a young lady who encountered so much along the roadway of life, it is no wonder her love for God intensifies with each new day.

To my wife and my best friend who loves God with all of her being, I pray that this book will bring in a harvest of souls who would like to experience a relationship with Jesus Christ.

I love you more than words can say.

Your husband,
John House

INTRODUCTION

*I*t was a beautiful summer morning, and while I was looking out of my bedroom window, I noticed the birds were singing their songs of happiness and contentment to the Lord. The wind was blowing gently through the trees, creating a coolness that was so necessary on this warm day. The flowers of my mother's garden had opened their petals and seemed to be bowing to the Lord in thankfulness for a new day. Little insects were dashing around in the soil, as though hiding from the heat of the sun. Movement and noise were everywhere, and thankfulness was present in the atmosphere. It all made me realize that God our creator was responsible for this beauty. I was suddenly very aware that all creation showed signs on this day that there was someone bigger than it to thank for all of this. Yes there was someone bigger, and He was the God of the universe, full of grace and power.

However there was something very different about this summer morning of peacefulness and contentment. It was suddenly interrupted by a feeling of desperation as I clutched the sides of my bed in urgency, trying to take each breath with much difficulty. You see, I had chronic asthma, and there was no hope for me. This seemed to change the atmosphere somewhat and echo a tone of despondency throughout the air to a wonderful family in a country many, many thousands of miles away—South Africa. This day was definitely different, as I was given the news that I had only one year to live.

Chapter 1

BORN TO LIVE AND NOT DIE

I was born in East London, South Africa to young Christian parents who loved me very much. They raised me in the admonition of the Lord, and my dad was a man of faith and instilled that in me from a young age. My mother was an organist in our local church and had an insatiable love for music and the Word of God, so both of my parents taught me to live in all holiness. I was a premature baby, born at seven months and only weighing four pounds. Due to being premature, my lungs were undeveloped, so at the age of three years old I was diagnosed with chronic asthma. As far as medical science was concerned, this diagnosis was inevitable as there was asthma on both sides of my family. As the firstborn, I became a target for this terrible disease. Therefore I had a long road to travel to becoming a healthy child, but God had another plan for my life. My parents did not give up on me; my dad had faith that the Lord would restore my lungs and make me strong and whole. My mom also knew that Jesus was our healer and trusted God for the impossible. I had wonderful grandparents who loved me and stayed at my side day and night. They also believed God would send my miracle. I had so many people praying for me.

As I grew older I became gradually worse, and finally at the age of nine years old, I became bed-ridden with three doctors on call, as my body became weaker and I began to have terrible trouble breathing as my lungs became worse. I continued to fight for my life daily. I missed a lot of school during this time. I used to listen to the children playing outside at dusk and heard them laughing and having a good time. So many times I wished I was outside with them, but I realized I could not endure the night air and the humidity, as it would make it even harder for me to breathe. I became very ill, but even at this age I had faith that Jesus could heal me, and my parents had also told me that He could do miracles as He had done in the days of the Bible. He healed so many in those days, therefore I knew beyond a shadow of a doubt that He was able to heal me as well. The Word of God says in Hebrews 13:8, "Jesus Christ the same yesterday, and today and forever," so if He healed yesterday, He heals today and will heal in the future. He does not change, and His Word does not return void. His word will always stand. The Psalmist said in Psalm 119:89,"Forever, O LORD, Thy word is settled in heaven." Somehow I knew there was a purpose for my life, and God had recorded all my comings and goings. I knew that I was fearfully and wonderfully made and that my destiny was in His great hands.

The suffering became very intense, as I was having terrible trouble breathing. At times I would even attempt to scrape the walls and pull on my pajama jacket because I felt like I was in a gas chamber, and I did not know what to do. My mom tied pieces of cloth tightly around my head, as the headaches were getting worse from my coughing. She also tied cloth tightly around my chest at my request because my lungs ached so much from the difficult breathing. I was also sleep deprived, so I constantly sat up in a bed with pillows propped around me to try to ease the suffering. I had long hair, and eventually the doctor told my mom to cut it, as all my strength was going into the growing of my hair, and at that time I needed all the strength that I could find. I then developed acne all over my face due to all the medications I was given, which I eventually became immune to. I also had repeated injections every day to help me breathe, but nothing helped. I became very desperate, and my dad became desperate as well as he exhausted a lot of his finances to try to make me well. My mom would help me out of bed and take me outside, sometimes around two in the morning, to see if I could have some ease in my breathing, but instead I would collapse into her arms, and she would have to help me back into bed. Through this all they still believed that God in His great mercy would heal me.

My dad bought me a tape recorder and placed it next to my bed. He gave me a tape of Reverend Oral Roberts preaching on the fourth man in the fire. He told the story of the three Hebrew children, Shadrach, Meshach, and Obednego being thrown into the fiery furnace because they would not bow to King Nebuchadnezzar but only to the God of Israel. They were not even touched by the flames, and their clothes were not burnt, because there was someone walking in the fire like unto the Son of God.

I knew throughout my fiery furnace that God would finally show up. I played the tape over and over again until my faith became strong, and I just knew that the Lord was going to heal me. I heard that Reverend Roberts as a young man was dying from tuberculosis and that God had miraculously healed him, so my faith increased each time I heard him preaching and testifying to God's healing power, especially when I heard him say repeatedly that God was a good God. I believed that He was good and that one day He would heal me as well. The other tape my dad gave me to listen to was the testimony of Betty Baxter, who was born to Nazarene parents. Betty had been born in a fetal position, arthritic in all her bones and joints. She stayed in this fetal position in a bed with her head touching her feet and having no hope. She was unable to wear clothes because she could not move any part of her body. I recall being a teenager and listening to her describing the miracle that God did for her during her bedridden state.

I will try to tell you what I can remember of her story to the best of my ability. Betty called her mother into the room and told her that she had received a vision from the Lord and that He was coming to heal her at three in the afternoon. She also received the words "with God all things are possible," Matthew

19:26. Her mother proceeded to tell her that, the night before, the Holy Spirit had given her the same verse.

On the day that the Lord was supposed to heal her, a small white cloud came into the house and moved all the way into Betty's room. It came close to her, and God began to heal her body. Many people were present, and the news media were watching for what they thought God could not do. Suddenly it sounded like gunshots as every bone in her body unlocked, straightened, and popped back into place. You see, Betty had so much faith in her miracle that she asked her mother to buy her a new dress and shoes so that she could go to church. So when the popping of each bone and joint stopped, she stood up and said, "Mama go get my dress."

My, what a healing Jesus. This woman of God touched my life with her testimony. One day she came to my city, and I decided to go and listen to her one evening, and there she was—healthy and strong with her family. I had been playing her tape daily to build my faith so that I could also receive my healing through the visitation of the Holy Spirit.

Chapter 2

A VERY SPECIAL VISIT FROM THE HOLY SPIRIT

I received the Lord into my heart at seven years old, under the ministry of Betty Baxter, who was very influential in my life. In an auditorium the night that Betty was giving her testimony, I walked to the front of the church, and it was then that I suddenly was visited by the Holy Spirit. He immediately touched my heart, and I began to weep uncontrollably in the presence of an Almighty God. I remember that night so clearly, and I remember my very special visitor who changed my life forever. I have never been the same since I accepted my precious Jesus into my heart. When the Lord visits you, your life changes and you are never the same. Believe me, when His presence envelops your life, you will be filled with joy. At that moment you are in such awe that it fills you with great love and tremendous appreciation for Him because He chose to die on the cross of Calvary for you and take all your sins upon Him so that you can go free. What an awesome God we serve. My life was never the same, and now as I grow older I am blessed with three wonderful sons and a wonderful husband who love the Lord with all their hearts. You see, getting married and having three healthy sons was not supposed to happen, as the enemy tried to destroy my life at a young age. He tried to destroy me in every way, but I had a very special visitor one morning

Special Visits

Many days as I grew older I enveloped myself in God's presence, and many times He paid me special visits, and I would communicate with Him daily. I knew that if He paid me enough visits to my bedroom while I was bedridden, I would learn all about Him. Then as I strived to become like Him and love Him more each day, He would heal my body. He let me know to not have fear and that He was in total control of my destiny. He told me that He made every part of my body, so why should I worry as He had everything under His control. He told me that He was overseeing my situation and to put my trust in Him. He spoke to me clearly, starting when I was a child, and I always enjoyed listening, because many a time snares were set for me by the enemy, and He told me that the enemy wanted to take my life but that His glory would be revealed.

I realized that He was the Lord, strong in battle, and that He would go to war for me. I also realized then that He was not going to allow me to die but that I would get well and declare the works of the Lord. He impressed upon me my duty to read the Word of God and not for it to gather dust because I would be laying him aside, and that would be rejecting the very one who is in control of my life. He made me aware that all things were possible with Him. Oh, how I loved these special visits from the Holy Spirit

Becoming Weaker:

After the many visits with my precious Savior, my body became weaker. My breathing became worse, and I became very ill, but I knew by an unmistakable knowledge that my very special visitor would heal me right on time. I have always believed the Lord is never late; He is always on time. Let us look at the story of Lazarus in John 11: 25 where Jesus says, "I am the resurrection, and the life: he that believeth in me, though he were dead, yet shall he live." Lazarus of Bethany became sick and died and was dead for four days when Jesus arrived. Martha went to Jesus and told him that if He had been there, her brother would not have died. The Lord told Martha that he would rise again and continued to tell Martha that He was the resurrection and the life. Jesus, in John 11:43, cries with a loud voice, "Lazarus come forth." Lazarus was bound hand and foot with grave clothes, and his face was bound with a napkin. Jesus said to them, "Loose him and let him go."(John 11:44)The Lord raised Lazarus from the dead, and his death was for the glory of God.

I also believed in my heart that when the Resurrected Christ would heal me it would be for His glory and that He would be right on time. My parents prayed continuously for my healing, and I held onto my faith everyday that God would finally heal me. By now I weighed about seventy-five pounds and was getting more and more sleep deprived because of the labored breathing I was experiencing. My mom and dad took turns sleeping in my room each night to watch over me, as my condition was becoming more serious. The suffering became very intense, and many times in my human frailty I wanted the Lord to take my life, but that was not His plan.

Chapter 3

MY NEED FOR A MIRACLE

The days and nights became very long as I sat in a bed unable to sleep or even eat properly. My heavy breathing was so intense that I was suffocating every minute. My lungs ached from the hard breathing, and I had severe headaches from the coughing, which was very uncontrollable most of the time. My parents propped pillows around me, and I sat up in bed unable to breathe. In fact everything that my parents tried to do to make me comfortable did not work. I was very sick and becoming worse. I needed a miracle, as I became more sleep deprived and lost a lot of weight rather suddenly, and I became skin and bones.

A 10:00a.m. Appointment:

My Aunt Sheena had a very special faith for my healing. She believed that God could do the impossible and so did I, so we arranged to make an appointment with the Lord at 10:00a.m. every morning. We never broke this appointment once we started, and we believed that if we continued to talk to Him, He would see our consistency and would finally grant me my healing. We took the heavens by force every morning, regardless of everything that would try to stop our appointment with the Lord. Aunt Sheena was a wonderful lady; it did not matter how many things she was doing at home, whether it was laundry or dishes or even vacuuming the floors, when I called her to come to our appointment, she left everything to come and pray with me. My uncle and my aunt lived next door to us, so that made it easier for her to come right over for our appointment with God. You see the Lord honors an appointment with Him. He loves when we pull away from the cares of this life and spend time in His presence; after all He created us for His glory and to worship Him. We continued to worship Him every day, and our faith became stronger as we both believed that the Lord was able to heal me.

As we touched heaven, the presence of the Lord entered the room daily. We did not see Him, but we felt him. Sometimes it seemed like He was walking in the room, His presence was so strong.

Distractions:

Distractions came many times, but we both stayed focused on what we wanted God to do. The enemy would tell us that God would never heal me, but we did not listen to him. Things would get so tough, and sometimes life seemed so rough, but we just called upon the name of Jesus each time. His name calms the biggest storm, and His name brings life instead of death, and I needed the life of the Word of God to hold onto during this time.

There were so many times that I thought my life was over, but instead I whispered His name daily, and His name would bring me such peace in my sickly state. I knew He was the Alpha and Omega, the beginning and the end, and that He was my rock in times of trouble and my refuge in the midst of the storm. God cares about us very much. He is the all-seeing eye of the universe. He even knows when the sparrow falls. If He cares for the little sparrow, He cares for us as well. My grandparents continued to pray for me each day and trust the Lord as well for my healing. One morning I heard someone praying really loud at about four-thirty in the morning. I got out of bed in my weak state and proceeded to the kitchen, where the voice was coming from. There was my precious grandpa, praying to the Lord as though he had entered the throne room of a King. I stood listening, eyes set on him, and I was so amazed I felt God all over again while he was praying. I was only a child at the time, but somehow my grandpa made such an impact upon me that I was more aware than ever that God had my comings and goings in the palm of His hand.

We continued to believe the Lord for my miracle for many years, and I only became worse. So many times I repeatedly tried to scrape the walls, yelling out, "I can't breathe, I can't breathe!" As a teenager who was very ill, I did not know that nothing could work as my lungs were shutting down, and they were shutting down fast. I needed a miracle from the Lord desperately.

After years of much suffering, being unable to breathe, and my heart becoming weaker every day, the doctor made his usual visit. Somehow I knew that something was very different about this day. He told my parents to make me comfortable, and that I had one year to live. I knew that I was dying because your heart can only take so much labored breathing for so long. This diagnosis caused me to reach up to the heavens one more time and ask the Lord to have mercy upon me. You see, I may have gotten discouraged with my illness off and on, but do not forget that when my faith kicked in I became bold, and I knew then that there was hope and that hope would change everything, as Jesus is our hope.

You see the name of Jesus is so dear to me; it brings joy to those who are sad, and it is like a pure breath of fresh air, and it is more precious than gold. I fell in love with Jesus throughout my suffering; in fact He became my best friend and my very special visitor.

Chapter 4

A GLIMPSE OF FUTURE GIFTS INTO THE PROPHETIC

During my suffering at the age of nine years old, my sweet baby brother went home to be with Jesus when he was only eighteen months old. This devastated me, as I loved him with all my heart. I used to look after him since I was the eldest daughter, and I loved taking care of him because he was so precious. I would spoil him so much in every way, and some nights my mother and I would sit at the fireplace knitting him sweaters of all colors. During this time I was becoming very sick from the asthma, and intervals of healthy breathing became less and less common.

My brother Ashley was born with a weakness in his heart. As he grew older he started the habit of lifting his hand while bending his fingers in and out of his palm and would say "bye, bye." He did this a lot, and "bye, bye" was the first word that he said. This bothered us and me especially as I always wondered if he was telling us that he was leaving soon. I came to the realization that God had truly blessed our family when he graced our lives with Ashley.

I had a glimpse of a future gift as God started talking to me prophetically at a young age.He let me know that Ashley was not going to stay for long. I did not share this with my family because I knew it would upset them. I just communicated with the Lord and prayed for him.

When it came time for him to have his smallpox vaccination, his arm became infected, and inspite of this the doctor still administered his booster shots. Because of him having a weak heart and his immune system being down, he could not fight all of the germs that were administered to him. We still do not know what he died from. He suddenly had trouble breathing and was rushed to the hospital. In the meantime my ability to glimpse the future, which I believed God was placing upon me, became stronger. When I asked my mother while he was leaving if he was coming back home, her reply to me was "yes," but in my heart I knew he would not return.

I was told that when he reached the hospital he became worse and started to go into convulsions because he could not breathe. The only relief he experienced was when he looked into a certain corner of the room and smiled. My mother believed it was because he saw someone, possibly an angel. When he looked away he would convulse again. My little brother went through so much suffering we could not understand it all, but we knew that God would stand with our family through this major storm. My mother ran out of the room to get help as he was getting worse, when suddenly the doctor walked up to her and told her that Ashley had passed. Although she is a woman of God, this was one of the biggest storms she ever found herself in.

My dad rushed home to tell me the bad news, but because I had already had a glimpse into the future from God, I told my dad that I knew that the Lord had already taken Ashley home. My dad was surprised at what I told him, but he also knew that God's hand was upon my life, and he continued to believe that I was born for a purpose.

The Lord prepared my mother before Ashley's death by giving her a song that she found in one of her Christian song books—"He Doeth All Things Well." I remember clearly that she called me over to the piano and told me that she wanted me to hear this song with such special words that God had given her. This song was given to her way in advance of Ashley's passing, so I again had a glimpse into the prophetic when I realized that God knew what He was doing, because He does do all things well.

The memories were the hardest to bear, because while walking through the house, we would find some of his little toys that we thought we had already put away so that my mom would not notice them. Somehow there were always more and more memories. One day I opened the kitchen cabinet, and there was his little sandal next the butter dish with his fingerprints in the butter. He loved to lick the butter from his little fingers. I believe that was the hardest thing for me to see at the time, because I really loved my little brother so much.

We prepared for the funeral, and he was so loved that he had 144 wreaths. During the funeral my mother played the organ while under such grief, and she told us that she felt like someone took her hands and played the organ for her. We knew that God had done this. A very good friend sang one of our favorite songs, "We'll Talk it Over in the Bye and Bye," and somehow we knew that we would talk it over with Jesus one day.

When we got to the graveside everyone was crying and sobbing, so when the coffin was lowering, hopelessness came over me, and it became final right then and there that I would never see my little brother again in this life. I knew, however, that I would see him in heaven because the Word of God says in 1Thessalonians 4:13 "that we do not sorrow even as others which have no hope."

The pastor called out to my mom as the casket lowered and said, "Stop crying and sing with me 'God Be With You till We Meet Again.'" The glory of the Lord descended that day as my mother lead the crowd gathered in worship. This I have never forgotten as long as I live. As she sang with such intensity and such an anointing, she knew beyond a shadow of a doubt that she would see her baby Ashley again.

Sometimes we are not aware of why God gives us songs in the night, so He blessed me later on in life with the words of a chorus: "Touch me and I will be healed, touch me and I will be healed, touch me and I will be healed. Pour out your power and glory on me, touch me and I will be healed."

There was a healing that happened that day as we sang "God Be with You till We Meet Again," so I know I will have the joy of seeing my brother Ashley again because I trust the Lord no matter what, because He knows what's best for me.

God told me from a young age, as I took a glimpse into the future gifts that He wanted to bestow upon me, that if I would take of His glory and surround myself with it, it would be a protection from many a storm that I would encounter along the way that would stop my mind from being focused on Him. Praise the Lord for a glimpse into the future. It changed my life at nine years old.

Chapter 5

A DIVINE VISIT FROM JESUS

$\mathscr{B}$y now I was so sick that I needed a major miracle from the Lord. As I became worse I continued to speak to the Lord regardless of how poorly I felt. I realized by now that I needed him more than ever. I knew when He went to Calvary that He took thirty-nine stripes by the Roman soldiers, which were for my healing. The Word of God says in Isaiah 53:5, "But He was wounded for our transgressions, He was bruised for our iniquities: the chastisement of our peace was upon Him; and with His stripes we are healed."

I continued to depend on the Lord through all of my suffering. One evening I told Mom to go and sleep with Dad and have a good night's rest, as she needed it, and I would be all right by myself. I told her I wanted to talk to Jesus and that I had some things to cover with Him. She continued to worry about my wellbeing but eventually left me as I requested. It was at about midnight that I called out to God and told Him just how bad I felt and that if He would find it in His heart to heal me from this terrible disease, that would be great. Since I was only fourteen years old, I told Him that since I gave him my heart, He was obligated to heal me. I also made a promise to Him that if He would heal me, I would become a missionary among the tribes in South Africa, and as I grew older I would help people with their problems, come what may. I knew that I was born with tremendous compassion for people that has carried through my life. I just did not want anyone to hurt from the enemy, and I knew that he came to kill, steal, and destroy. I told God that I would love to teach Bible School and become a preacher and teacher as well. I continued to tell Him that if He would heal me, I would serve Him the rest of my life and that He would be number one in everything I do.

After my prayer, I waited with faith that God heard me and that He would come through for me no matter what. I somehow knew that I would not die but would live to declare the works of the Lord. (Psalm 118:17)

Jesus Walks in:

Around two hours after I prayed, I heard someone enter my room. My hair stood up on my arms, and I had goose bumps as I realized that someone very special had just walked in. I heard the footsteps as they came closer and closer to my bed. I did not see anyone, but I sure heard Him and felt Him. There is something about Jesus when He enters a room. You know it beyond a shadow of a doubt. While I was having this encounter, my grandmother, who lived with us, came to the restroom across from my bedroom and suddenly stopped in the doorway. She looked above my head as though she saw something. She did not talk to me but stared at me and shook her head and then left and told my mom that she believed that God had healed me. She saw a white light above my head that she said illuminated the whole bedroom.

As the footsteps came closer and stopped at my bed, my lungs opened up, and I fell into my first deep sleep after many years. I slept so soundly that my mom did not want to wake me. I woke myself up at 8:30a.m. and leapt out of bed and opened my Bible to Isaiah 58:8, "Then shall thy light break forth as the morning, and thine health shall spring forth speedily: and thy righteousness shall go before thee; the glory of the LORD shall be thy reward."

I looked right at that verse, and it had become a reality right then and there. The Word of God is so powerful; I believe it with all of my heart.

I ran with excitement to the kitchen where my mom was cooking lunch, and I proceeded to tell her that God had healed me and that I was no longer having trouble breathing. She continued to tell me that grandma, who did not believe God could heal me, told her that she was sure I received my healing. Well I sure did, and I was so thankful and overwhelmed with what God had done for me.

Almost immediately my strength started coming back. Each day I became stronger, and what a milestone that was, as I was so weak before God healed me. As my body became stronger, my mind became sharper, and although I was only fourteen years of age, my goals to fulfill God's plan became my total focus. I was so excited because I knew that He had a wonderful plan for my life and that my destiny was in

His great, powerful hands. I knew that once you leave your destiny in God's hands and work right alongside Him, you accomplish what He wants to accomplish in your life, and it becomes more real to you daily. My future became more real to me everyday, so I decided to walk in His footprints and together with my Lord; I would find the right path and place where He wanted me to go. As I said earlier, I had a compassion for souls, so I did not enjoy anyone hurting or being sad. I always wanted to fix it, so here I was with compassion and love for others I could not explain, except I knew it was deep inside my DNA and that God would use me to help many a dying soul and teach them about a Savior who loved them unconditionally.

Chapter 6

AFTER THE MIRACLE

After my miracle I continued to visit with the Holy Spirit.

As a teenager I had a tremendous love for the Lord that I could not explain. No one could change how I felt about Him. I just knew that He was my Shepherd and now that I was healed, He was able to direct me on the rest of my journey. My favorite verse was in Proverbs 3:6, "In all thy ways acknowledge Him and He would direct thy paths."

Going Back to School:

Since I had lost so much schooling, my parents decided to take me to a Catholic School where I could receive special care with my studies. They knew that the nuns specialized in helping students, so they thought that this would be a great school for me where I would get special attention. They put me up a grade and told me if I worked hard I would catch up to the other students and graduate alongside them in standard ten. We in South Africa call each grade a standard, so our standard ten is grade twelve in America.

I worked very hard and came forth in standard eight in my class. In the meantime I had made friends with a Chinese girl whose name was Elizabeth. She was very smart, and everything came to her naturally, while I had to work hard to make my standards. When I became fourth out of about fifty students, she came third in our class. I used to tease her that one day I would pass her up and become first in my class. I continued to work hard, and with the help of the nuns, I managed to come third in standard nine, and Elizabeth came in second in our class. I continued to tell her that I was going to work very hard and that I was going to pass her up the last year when we graduated. Guess what? I came first in standard ten, and she could not believe it. She went to the teacher and asked her if she could check our marks because she did not believe that I passed her. The teacher continued to tell her that I passed her by quite a number of points.

We continued to be great friends, so when prize giving was celebrated, which was held once we graduated, my name was called each time, and I received most of the trophy cups that evening. Elizabeth stood behind me and said, "I cannot believe you did so well." All I thought about was how God created a miracle in my life by healing me and now helping me excel in each of my classes. I was not a proud person; I was only grateful for the Lord helping me with each class as He always instilled in me that He would guide and direct my paths.

During my time at the Catholic School, I always wanted to help the nuns as well as some of the students with the help of the Holy Spirit. In fact I became close to some of the nuns, and they wanted me to teach them the Bible. Now do not forget that all they knew was the Catholic Bible, so sometimes during my lunch hour I would teach the nuns the King James Version of the Bible in the music room. They were so intrigued with what I was teaching them that they would alert me when Mother Superior was on her way, and they would hide me under the piano to protect me each time. It was such a privilege to have the ability to expound the Word of God to the Catholic nuns.

In the schools in South Africa, we had a Head Girl as well as a Vice Head Girl over the whole school. The rule of thumb was that they were supposed to be Catholics. However Roslyn, one of my friends who was a Catholic, was made Head Girl, and I was made Vice Head Girl even though I was not a Catholic. I have to say I had a lot of respect from the nuns; some came to me with their problems, and I always tried to answer with the help from the Holy Spirit. There was a special pretty little nun who was much younger than the rest. One day she came to me and asked me if I knew why she was so unhappy. I had no clue but then the Holy Spirit alerted me that she had mentioned the Hail Mary numerous times, that she had said them so much that they did not mean anything to her anymore; the Rosary, she continued to tell me, had no more meaning as she continued to chant it.

I told her that the reason for that was that it had become a ritual and that it had no more meaning. I told her that God wanted her to have a relationship with Him, not tradition and ritualism. She told me that she was in her eighth year and that this was the year for her to make the decision to leave the convent or stay. I told her that the best advice to give her was that she alone had to make the decision. If she was that unhappy, how could she spend the rest of her life bound to that? I continued to tell her that I believed she would make the best decision with the help of the Holy Spirit. After I graduated, I received a letter in the mail from her, telling me that she had left the convent and was working in another state as a secretary and was dating a priest that had also left the religious life. I was so thankful that she chose the right path for her life. She was very special and loved the Lord, which is why she went to the convent in the beginning. This became a new day for her after that decision. I have to say the nuns became my friends and were very helpful to me during my school years.

After Graduation:

After graduation I decided to go to teachers' training college. I was to take a three-year course to be a kindergarten teacher. I made all the plans to further my career, but somehow on my way to college, my very special visitor told me that I needed to pursue going to Bible school instead. I went through with my studies for three months at college and was very unhappy and expressed this to my parents at the time. Eventually they brought me back home and realized that I had a calling on my life and that I needed to pursue what I felt the Holy Spirit was telling me.

I took a job at a bank in our local town and worked there for a while, at the same time pursuing God daily concerning the plans He had for me. I believe that feeling like I had to teach was nothing other than the Holy Spirit instilling in me that I should teach Bible school instead. I eventually found out that it had nothing to do with being a kindergarten teacher, but instead I should be a teacher of God's word, which had been my passion from a young age. I always believed that He would open doors for me to teach Bible school somehow so that I could make a difference in many people's lives.

Chapter 7

MEETING THE LOVE OF MY LIFE

My parents introduced me to a very good-looking man called Reuben who was a minister in South Africa. He was tall, had dark hair, beautiful eyes, and was very handsome. I was immediately attracted to him. He used to visit our home frequently, as he loved my parents very much. As he frequented our home, I noticed that he loved the Lord with all his heart, and this made me excited because I also loved the Lord, and He was a very big part of my life. The attraction grew and grew on his part as well as mine, and eventually we fell in love with each other.

In the meantime my dad started going to a photographic studio in our local town called Queenstown and met the owners of the business. It was a family-owned business, and my dad met the son, Eric, whom he felt comfortable with developing all his pictures of the ministry for him. He came home that day and said that he would like me to meet the son. I was totally confused because I was already in love with Reuben, so I was very reluctant.

I needed a portrait taken of myself, so I went to his photography studio. He took my picture and did a tremendous job, as he was the best photographer in Queenstown, South Africa. He placed my picture in the window, so he made me feel very special. I noticed that every time I walked into his store, he would get rather excited to see me. I did not want to encourage him, as I was so much in love with Reuben, so I backed off. However my father encouraged Eric to pursue a relationship with me because he believed that he would be a better provider than Reuben. Any good parents would want the best for their children, but I wanted to follow my heart. I ended up marrying Eric out of respect for my father.

Reuben approached me one day and said, "Your dad wants you taken care of financially, and I can't take care of you like the photographer can," so in order to not offend my parents, we decided to go our separate ways. I told him money was not everything, and that would be the hardest decision of my life. I was a daughter who always obeyed my parents in every way, whether I understood it or not. I was naïve and thought they knew something I did not know, so I was hurt very badly in the process. I ignored my feelings all the way and decided to marry someone I did not really love. Eric the photographer was a very good person, but when you get married you have to love that person very deeply.

We were affiliated with a church overseas that my dad had found in America while pursuing God's plan for his life. This church had a woman preacher who would periodically come and visit us at our home in South Africa. When she arrived my dad would always give her the red-carpet treatment.

The minister from America was visiting us one day when my new boyfriend Eric and I decided to take her to a restaurant in our local town. She also told us both in front of each other that he was my future husband, so when I left the restaurant I asked her a very important question. I wanted her to explain why God would put two people together when one of them did not love the other like they should. Her reply was he is the right man for you and that God had told her so. She went on to say that I would learn to love him. This really bothered me, but I also knew God's voice and somehow felt very uneasy about the relationship. In the meantime my boyfriend did not give me much time to be alone, as he was always around because he loved me very much. One of the things that concerned me the most was that he was not saved, so one day I walked around the block with him telling him the plan of salvation, and praise the Lord, he gave his heart to the Lord when we got home. I believe this decision changed his life forever by sending him in the right direction.

I was always a girl who listened to my parents and thought they knew best, so Eric and I started dating. He pursued his relationship with Christ and developed a great love for the Word of God.

Getting Married:

We became engaged and decided to get married, while I was still fighting my feelings. I believed that God would change my heart, and I asked Him to help me fall in love with my fiancé every day, as I did not want to hurt him. In fact I shared this with him and told him that he was a very special person and that he had to give me time to fall in love with him.

My dad came to me one day and asked me if I wanted to have a big wedding or if I would prefer money instead. I told him that I wanted a big wedding, something that I could remember; so plans were made for a large wedding in Queenstown, South Africa. My mom worked hard and furiously to make it a great success. She was a very talented woman, so she made my beautiful wedding dress, the bridesmaids' dresses, the headgear, and even dyed the shoes for each bridesmaid and flower girl. She cooked all the food for approximately 300 people, and my dad organized the wedding to be in the Town Hall in Queenstown because of the number of the guests. We agreed that mom would even play the wedding march and also sing at our wedding—my, what a lady. We also arranged for a family friend who was a minister to officiate the ceremony.

The Officiating Minister Cancels Shortly before the Wedding:

I received a phone call one afternoon from the minister who was going to marry us, telling me his car had broken down and that he would not be able to make it. He said that as he had to drive many hours to get to Queenstown, he would never be in time for the wedding. I immediately panicked and did not know who to call to take his place. After I thought it through, I decided that there was only one option, and that was to call my ex-boyfriend to officiate the wedding. He immediately told me that this would be the hardest thing for him to do, but because it was me he would drive down to be in time for our wedding. He arrived the night before and stayed at our home. While I was packing my suitcase for the honeymoon, he stood in the doorway of my bedroom and told me that this was not right and that he was supposed to marry me instead. We spoke about eloping, but he did not want to hurt my parents, and neither did I as my mom had gone all out for this wedding.

The Wedding Takes Place:

I could not sleep all night because of my feelings and because I was working so hard to make this wedding a success. I finally put my wedding dress on and reluctantly got into the car that would take me to the Town Hall where the wedding was to take place. In fact I was fifteen minutes late for my wedding, and my fiancé was pacing the floor. My dad led me to the front and placed me alongside my fiancé, and I realized I was looking into the eyes of someone who loved me very much. The only thing different was that in front of me was the minister whom I loved dearly, and he was getting ready to officiate our wedding.

What a state of confusion I found myself in, but I knew I could not hurt my fiancé and that God would help me with this marriage. Reuben did a great job, except he mentioned divorce on my wedding day, which I did not like, so I was crying under my veil. He was also the master of ceremonies and decided to tell 300 people that instead he should be taking me down the isle on my wedding day. You see, sometimes the Holy Spirit gives us sign after sign, and He guides us so many times, but we do not always listen to His voice. I tried to ignore everything that affected my emotions and focused on marrying my fiancé. We had a beautiful wedding, and we were both very proud of my parents, who went all out to make it a success.

After the wedding Reuben gave us a Bible as a gift, wishing us the best. I have never seen him since. In fact one of my family members saw him after many years, and he told her that he was still in love with me. I heard that he finally got married and had some children, as I was told, so I was not sure about that. However I did not make any effort to find him, as I had made a new commitment to my new husband and that is what I believed God would have wanted from me.

Chapter 8

A CHANGE FROM ONE LIFE TO ANOTHER

We left South Africa after selling all that we had and set out for a new life and destiny in America. We both knew that God had arranged for us to go to America to fulfill our calling from God. We then taught Bible school and continued to find the correct path that the Lord was leading us through. We left everything like Abraham not knowing where he was going, but being a man of faith, he trusted the Lord totally. Therefore we left in faith as well and arrived in a country we knew nothing about, except that we knew in our hearts that God had made a way for us to come to America.

We lived on $50.00 a week, which the church gave us along with a place to stay. The living quarters were not anything to write home about; we did not even have a bed. We were given one eventually, but it was not in good shape. Things became harder everyday as we encountered even more problems with our living conditions. We ventured out in search of what God had planned for our lives. Somehow we knew He would make a way for us if we would just trust Him. The thing that confused me was that the minister of this church was always treated well when she came to our country, but somehow this was not the case with us. God had another plan for us later, as I had called the church and asked for help, so the situation was redeemed. A very special sister from the church we were affiliated with removed us immediately and placed us in her wonderful guest house.

After learning the Word of God and even teaching Bible school, we became ministers of the Gospel and missionaries to South Africa.

My Promise:

I remembered promising the Lord that if he healed me, I would help many people and that I would even become a missionary and work with the tribes in South Africa to tell them about Jesus, so we left America and headed back to our country to fulfill what God wanted for our lives.

We bought a jeep that got ten miles to the gallon, and I would sometimes go into the Transkei, which was too far away from Queenstown, South Africa where we were missionaries. It was hilly and rugged, with woody vegetation and few roads. In fact I used to make my own roads to reach my destination. The Transkei was predominately populated by the Xhosa tribe, who specialized in farming mostly with sheep and cattle, and who made beadwork and pottery. The man would sit with his big heavy blanket outside his mud hut, while wearing his large hat and smoking his pipe. The woman would do all the gardening and grow all the corn and the beans, and whatever else they decided to plant for their livelihood. Their little children did not have a lot to play with, but they were so thankful for what they had that it touched a cord inside of me that I have never forgotten. These people were so humble and appreciative for what they were given that they enjoyed life nonetheless.

The only thing that was missing was that someone had to tell them about Jesus, so we did just that.

Sometimes I was fearless, and many times I would go into the Transkei all alone. I did not have children yet, so my time was spent around the things of God, which became my passion. I would leave early in the morning and come back around four or so in the afternoon and would sometimes wonder how I would get home, as I was not aware of many parts of the Transkei. Somehow the Holy Spirit always directed me and I would make it home safely.

We met witch doctors and many a hungry soul who needed Jesus. In fact God led us to a witch doctor everyone was scared of, as they believed he put spells on people and mixed potions, which he told them could make them well. After we shared the gospel with him, he became a minister for us and threw off his witch doctor clothes and wore a suit, shirt, and tie, which was amazing as he now had a relationship with the God of the universe. He became a precious soul for Jesus.

We continued to evangelize the Transkei and Queenstown, South Africa, so we touched cultures for the Lord. One day we had a baptismal service for approximately 150 people of all races who were now saved by the blood of Jesus and wanted to fulfill the commandment of Baptism in Matthew 28:19 and Acts 2:38. "Then Peter said Repent and be baptized everyone of you in the Name of Jesus Christ for the remission of sins, and he shall receive the gift of the Holy Ghost."

The most amazing thing happened that day while we were baptizing them. The power of God hit them in such a way that we had to carry them out of the water and lay them on the banks of the river. They looked like dead people, but we knew that once we mentioned the name of Jesus it would have an effect on them, and they would never be the same again. They eventually moved and jumped up with excitement and told us what they had experienced. For one thing, we baptized them on a very cold winter day, and when we put them in the water and mentioned the name of Jesus, the water literally heated up and God's Holy Presence was felt among all. That was when I realized that I was born for a purpose and that my healing was not in vain. What an amazing day.

Chapter 9

THE AMAZING BIRTH OF MY SON GARRICK

$\mathcal{D}$uring the time we were missionaries in Queenstown, I became pregnant with my first child. We were very excited about this and prepared to welcome this special life with a lot of love. As the pregnancy progressed, I felt that I might die with this birth, and I relayed my concern to my family. They thought I was just scared since I had never had a baby before, and they continued to console me and tell me that everything would be all right. I knew better because the feeling became stronger and stronger, and the pregnancy became harder and harder as the baby was lying breach and had to be turned every so often by the doctor.

As the time came closer for me to have my son, the feeling became very strong, and I did not want to believe that I would die with this birth, so I continued to pray for my protection from the Lord that He would guide the doctors through the birth so that I would be fine. Once I put my trust in the Lord, I was at peace. In fact He prompted me to read Psalm 91:11 where it says, "For He shall give His angels charge over thee to keep thee in all thy ways." I kept this verse close to my heart daily.

Eventually at 2:30 one morning I realized I was going into labor, so I was rushed to the hospital right away. They monitored me during each contraction. Finally the contractions became two minutes apart and very, very painful. My mom had been through numerous pregnancies, so she had shown me how to breathe during each contraction, so I became quite a pro at breathing correctly during the contractions. In fact a nurse asked me if I had any other children because I was not screaming during the major pain I was experiencing.

The contractions that were two minutes apart kept on for thirty-two hours, and I became very ill as my heart was slowing down. I became numb as the baby was lying in a posterior position in the birth canal and was also lying on a nerve. While he tried to turn for birth, every two minutes I experienced awful pain.

They finally wheeled me into the labor ward the following day at three in the morning, and by now my body was so numb I told the nurse there was no way I could push the baby out. They rubbed me down with cans of Johnson's baby powder to increase my circulation. I needed help, so I asked the nurse on duty to call my doctor right away. The doctor believed that I might need a caesarian section, but he did not believe in taking the baby too soon, so he let me wait more hours, as he was going to do a caesarian as a last resort. I could not figure this one out as he was the gynecologist for all my mom's children as well and I trusted him. My father-in-law came into the labor ward for a few minutes, and when he saw me I looked so bad that he said, "Oh my God no," and he left. I knew if the doctor would not come soon that I was going to die. In the meantime I asked my husband to read Psalm 91:11 over and over, which he did. He read that verse so many times that I believe the Lord heard our prayers and responded to our faith and had everything under control.

I got worse and worse, and at 7:30a.m. I asked the nurse if she could call the doctor one more time, as

I felt I was not going to make it. I definitely needed surgery to remove the baby. She called him, but he only showed up at about 9:15a.m., so by the time he checked me over he was so shocked at the status of my body that he said loudly, "I do not care who is in surgery. This girl needs surgery right away, and we have to make it happen." I was wheeled into surgery right away, but I still had a peace about every thing. When you know the Holy Spirit, He gives you peace and comfort that is beyond anything you will ever know. The nurse wheeling me asked me how I could smile when I knew my condition was so serious. I told her that I knew the Lord was in charge of my life. When I got into surgery, I died right away.

I remember hurtling very fast down a tunnel of purple and blue colors, and I was traveling at such a speed that the tunnel became smaller and smaller until I reached the other side where there was light. I immediately told the Lord that if He wanted me to stay there, I would if He would take care of my husband and my baby son. When I surrendered to stay, He miraculously brought me back to life, and there were three doctors standing over me. One was the heart doctor with an oxygen mask over me, because at the time I was breathing very rapidly. They slapped my face and told me that they had not done the surgery yet, but that they were now going to take the baby out by caesarian. I was administered the anesthesia, and I went out knowing that God was in total control of my life. Our Son was born at 10:06 on a Sunday morning, and I was taken into recovery where I did not come around until about three in the afternoon that day.

My mom was in total shock to see what I looked like, as I had intravenous feeding in each arm, while at the same time I had black and blue bruises on my face from the doctor slapping me to make me come back to life. He sat on the bed across from me after I came out of recovery, and my mom asked him why I looked like I did. His answer was that he had to slap me because I died and eventually he gave me mouth to mouth, and that is how I came back to life. He suggested that if my family wanted to sue him that would be fair, as he waited too long to do the surgery that was so needed at the time. Of course we did not sue him as we were Christians and we knew that God had determined that I would not die but live and declare the works of the Lord. (Psalm 118:17)

Our son was healthy but had a terrible lump on the side of his head, which looked like an egg. It was not serious; it was a blood blister from him turning so many hours in the birth canal and hitting his head on the pelvic bone. We prayed about this and laid our hands upon his head every day and within six months it was gone. He remains a very smart child, so the difficult birth never affected him in the least. He has a fantastic brain and went into the Air Force and became a meteorologist, advising the pilots on favorable weather for flying the F16's. He has twenty-one years of service in the Air Force and many medals for his achievements. I believe that the enemy wanted to kill both of us because of our future, but he did not get it right as my son had to fulfill his destiny, and I had to let many people know about the Lord through my testimony. My God is a good God, may His name be praised.

Chapter 10

MY VERY SPECIAL VISITOR LEADS ME TO A DIVINE APPOINTMENT WITH A SALESMAN

We had moved from Queenstown, South Africa, and God had led us to Cape Town, South Africa where we were to assist my parents. One day while I was alone at home, I received a knock at my door. There before me stood a very tall gentleman dressed in a suit with a suitcase of some sort, and he asked me if I would be interested in seeing the clothes he was selling. I let him come in, as I always listened to the voice of the Lord as to what I should do. I somehow knew that it would be safe and that God sent him to my door. He told me his name was

Donald. He came into the living room when he suddenly said that it was very warm in my house. The air conditioner was on, and I knew that what he was feeling was the power of God. He asked me if I could give him a glass of water, I did, and then he said, "I just have to go." I thought it was rather strange that he had not shown me the clothes he was selling and that he would leave so soon. He proceeded to leave anyway, and that was when I told him that I needed to help him with his life, and that if he left he would be back knocking on my door. He left. You see, God showed me Donald's life before me; I knew he was on drugs and that he was trying to start a new life by being a salesman.

The Salesman Comes Back:

A week or so passed and there was another knock on my door. In front of me stood Donald, and this time he was dressed in casual clothes. He proceeded to tell me that he had been in a car accident and that his life was a mess and he needed a change. I invited him in again, but only this time he was very willing to let me help him. I led him to the Lord in prayer and prayed that God would release him from his addiction.

He got so excited after we prayed that he asked me if I would go and help a friend of his who was hooked on LSD and was standing on a street corner, high on drugs. I was in my mid thirties, so I said that I would. I took him with me to show me where his friend was. Don't forget that I had not known these men previously at all, and by now I knew that I was taking my life in my own hands. But I again heard the voice of the Lord like he had spoken to me so many times, and he told me to go ahead with what I was doing and that he would protect me. We drove into the heart of Cape Town, South Africa, and there on the sidewalk was standing a tall man. His hair was on his shoulders, and he was talking to himself and moving his hands quite a bit. I proceeded to get out of the car and walk toward him, with the power of God all over me. I asked him what his name was, and he told me he was called Hans. I asked him if he knew a man called Jesus. His reply was "I have heard of Him." He told me that if I could answer a question for him, he would listen to me but not otherwise.

With speech very slurred, he continued to tell me that while he was on a high he hallucinated that he was falling into a bottomless pit that was black and dark. He continued to fall, but when he thought there was no hope for him, something caught his fall that felt like a rock that scratched him. I told him that Christ was our rock and that He stopped his fall so that he would not go into utter destruction, because He had a plan for his life. He became so excited after I answered him that he wanted to know more about Jesus. I asked him if he wanted to go with Donald and me back to my home so I could pray with him. He did, so I drove Hans and Donald back to my home.

I continued to talk to Hans about his soul. I told him that if he would receive the Lord into his heart and make a commitment to Him, He would deliver him from his addiction. I told him that God was able to deliver him from his addiction without him having any withdrawals. He became very excited about that statement and said that he would believe God for his miracle.

I prayed for him, and he committed his life to the Lord and never had a withdrawal from drugs. After I took him and Donald home, my neighbor asked me quietly who I thought I had brought into my home. I replied, "Just two drug addicts." She continued to tell me about Hans, that he was the most dangerous drug addict in Cape Town and that he would stab people with a pocketknife as got off the bus because he was so high. I told her that he was no longer dangerous and that he would no longer be on any drugs. I just knew beyond a shadow of a doubt that God had done a tremendous miracle in his life in just a few minutes. She frowned at me and thought I was crazy. I proceeded to take them home anyway regardless of what she thought because I had heard from God.

My parents had a church in Cape Town, so Donald and Hans started coming to their church. Hans would get so excited during worship that he would lift his long arms to heaven and tell the Lord that he loved Him so much. It was beautiful to see what God had done in his life. I continued to pray for his slurred speech, and one day God healed him miraculously. He had a lot to be thankful for.

We made plans to visit America and study theology for three years, so I decided to leave my country with my husband. I bought a home in Jeffersonville, Indiana and lived there about twenty years. Hans had a calling on his life and also wanted to go to Bible school at the time, so he followed me to America, where he met one of my friends and finally married her. They had two children, and the eldest was a very heavenly child whom my children used to love to play with. The baby was also so very cute, but there was something about his eldest that sometimes made me feel like he was too special for this earth. I could not explain what I was feeling.

One evening when they were coming from Kansas City in their van carrying Christmas toys they had received from their parents, the electricity went out of the van and they had to pull over onto the side of the road until they got help. This was around 4:30 in the morning. In the meantime Hans's wife made two beds in the back of the van for the boys. The eldest continued to ask her not to put him by the back door of the van, in fact he begged her. It was like he felt something. She continued to tell him that she had to put his baby brother close behind the back window so she could watch over him, so because of that she had to make his bed by the back door. They were hit by a drunk driver, and he was flung out of the van into the air, and Hans ran toward him while he was falling onto the road. Hans cried out to the Lord and said, "Please do not take my child. I have served you for so many years now." He picked his son up, and he gave one breath and was gone. This was devastating to Hans, and at that point he did not know where his wife or the baby were as they were flung out of the van as well. He heard them crying and found them in a ditch with gasoline burns and an injury to his wife's head.

This was a terrible accident and the trouble was there was no one on the road at that time of the morning. God got them through this, so since Hans had bought a home around the corner from me in Indiana, he often came and talked with me about the things of God. One day we were sitting on my steps in front of the house, and I asked him if he ever thought of going back on drugs since he lost his son. It was quite a stupid question to ask him, because I knew God had delivered him from drugs years ago. He proceeded to tell me that he would never even think about it, and that he was all right with God taking his child, as he believed that he only loaned him for a season. He continued to tell me that he missed him terribly but thanked God for the chance he had of raising him during his time here. That was so touching to me, and I realized even more that I was serving a big God and that I was born for a definite purpose.

Chapter 11

GOD GUIDES US ON A VACATION WHERE HIS GLORY IS MADE KNOWN

We had been working very hard as missionaries in South Africa, and after we moved back to Cape Town, we needed a vacation, so we were invited by two of our friends, Betah and Timothy, to come and rest at their farm. They had a dairy farm that they owned in the Eastern Cape of South Africa near the Fish River. In fact we crossed the Fish River when we were on their farm and had fun doing it. We thought that would be a great time to get together and share the word of God with them, which they were excited to do. They were so hungry for the things of the Lord that we knew we had to go and visit them.

We set out on our journey by car. Their home was many, many miles from Cape Town. After we traveled for a number of hours, I started getting very sick on the road with terrible stomach cramps. They eased up every so often but started up again, but this time with unbearable pain. I had never experienced anything like this before. My husband was getting worried, as he had to stop at every rest stop on the way. I became worried as well, and I knew something was very wrong in my body. Somehow I have always learnt to trust the Lord in everything I do, so I knew that we had heard from heaven and this vacation was going to be special regardless of the pain I was experiencing.

We finally reached the farmhouse where our friends welcomed us with open arms. They knew I was sick and suggested that I make an appointment to see a doctor the following morning in Somerset East, approximately twenty-eight miles from their farm. I went for the appointment and the diagnosis was appendicitis. The doctor scheduled surgery right away. I wondered what God had in mind for me as now I had to go through surgery on vacation.

I had the surgery and everything went well, except I knew that the surgical cut the surgeon gave me, which was as long as a caesarian in those days, did not feel good. The doctor gave me an extensive cut on my stomach as he wanted to make sure that everything was all right inside my body and that the appendix had not poisoned my system as it was about to burst. I constantly cried and told him that blood was seeping out of the wound, and it was not healing like it should. In fact I had one son and they delivered him by caesarian, and that wound felt fine after surgery, except for the normal pain one experienced, so I knew this was not doing well. He told me that he could not open me up again, so I cried when I left the hospital as I knew that the wound was not right and the Lord told me that it had to be reopened to be repaired properly. I cried all the way back to the farm, and my husband asked me why I was so upset. I told him that my stomach did not feel good and that there was pressure behind the wound. I just knew there was something very wrong.

In the meantime we were due to leave the farm in a couple of days and drive back to Cape Town, South Africa. I had been gone so long because of the surgery and the recovery that we both knew that my parents needed us to help with God's work. Therefore we felt that it was imperative to go back home. We set out in the late afternoon, and as we reached the highway the car's motor started burning. Smoke was everywhere and the car stalled. In those days we did not have cell phones, and we were in such a remote area that there were not many cars on the highway at all. All we could do was sit and wait until help arrived. We prayed and God sent Timothy back to the highway to meet some new guests who were scheduled to visit them. He immediately noticed our dilemma and drove us back to the farm where we spent the night.

The following morning Timothy and my husband took the car in for repairs and were gone for a number of hours. In the meantime I developed an allergy from the pollen on the farm and sneezed constantly, which was not good for the scar, as I had clips in my stomach keeping it together. I suddenly let out a big sneeze and Betah noticed blood coming out of my stomach. We both panicked, so she immediately looked for the car keys to take me to the hospital, which was more than twenty miles away on dirt road. She realized there were no car keys as Timothy had taken the car to help my husband in the process of repairing ours. I continued to bleed even more, so she wrapped sheets around me to try to tie the blood off. Nothing helped. She called the doctor and asked for an ambulance to take me to the hospital. The doctor told her that I would die before they got there, and it would be quicker and a shorter distance for her to bring me to the hospital. When we did not know what to do, we prayed to God for a miracle and immediately after we prayed, Timothy and my husband walked in the door and they saw the dilemma. Timothy immediately carried me to the car and drove over twenty miles on a dirt road to the hospital. When we arrived at the hospital I was very weak, so he had to carry me into the emergency room. I stayed calm all the way, as I knew that God had my life in His wonderful hands.

The nurses tended to me and said they were going to get help for me. Unfortunately the help did not come right away, as the doctor was not sure what to do because he had not had a wound of this magnitude open up before. They knew that surgery was inevitable, so in the meantime I lost more blood and got weaker. My body started getting very cold from the loss of blood. I eventually told the nurse that I was not going to make it unless they did surgery right away. She went back to the doctor, and I was immediately wheeled into surgery. I knew that I needed a miracle, so I prayed before they put me under anesthesia. After the prayer I saw a vision of four warrior angels standing with swords at each point of my bed. I immediately was at peace when I went out under the anesthesia.

I came around after surgery feeling much better, and my stomach felt flat and had no more pressure. The doctor informed me that I was a miracle, as when they put me under for surgery I coughed and I tore everything open in my stomach, and the bleeding increased tremendously, and they did not know what to do. There was a blood clot from the previous surgery, and it was the size of my hand. He said all the doctors went to my aid to stop the bleeding. He said God was with them, and He must have guided their hands to repair the problem. I knew immediately that those angels I saw went to war for me because the enemy wanted to take me out, and God was not going to allow it because I was His child.

After I recovered I was invited to the home of the doctor who had done the surgery. He told me previously that he was to blame because he had not tied off the blood vessels correctly the first time he did the surgery. That was the reason I had felt so much pressure under the wound. He continued to share with me that I must have had great faith in the Lord, because he believed that if it had not been for that, I would have died. He had an organ in his living room that he wanted me to play. I played and sang the song "I wouldn't take nothing for my journey now; I've got to make it to heaven somehow." He was so impressed that God touched his life from that day forth. He believed that God sent me across his path so he could learn more about Him. He was a changed man after this happened.

Chapter 12

OUR LIVES TAKE A MAJOR TURN

After we came to America, we accepted an invitation to pastor a church in Evansville, Indiana. By now I had two little boys whose names were Garrick and Dayne. They were very precious to me and were somehow different in every way. Garrick always played with toy airplanes and somehow I knew that he would eventually go into the Air Force to fulfill his destiny. He did just that, and as I said earlier, he became a meteorologist. His commander was very intrigued one day when we were visiting him at the Air Force base. He told us that he would notice the slightest movement on the radar and know exactly what was going to happen in advance. I remain very proud of his achievements. He retired from the Air Force and continues to fulfill his destiny in California.

Dayne was the talker of the two and always liked puppies. Somehow I knew that he would have dogs later on in life, and in fact now he has four dogs. He became a vice president of a Sports magazine, and it was because he had the know-how to talk to the clients who would be the sponsors for the magazine. He has done very well and has worked hard at making a home for his family and continues to be very successful.

Lance, my youngest son, became an assistant manager at Winn Dixie Supermarket stores and was an entrepreneur in every way. He even placed a bubblegum machine outside the store that he bought and collected I believe $40.00–$60.00 a week. When he was around seven years old, he would buy the candy called Now and Later for 25cents and would sell each candy in the wrapping for a quarter a piece. He therefore made a profit regardless. He continues to be an entrepreneur and also has a job setting up blind people with their computers. Some of them are in wheelchairs, and Lance knows how to set up the lights in their homes according to their disabilities. What a gift he has. They have all done so very, very well.

The church did very well in Evansville, Indiana, and the Lord blessed us tremendously. After being successful pastors, we received a phone call one day asking us to come back to the home church in Indiana where our lives took a major turn. We both had to get jobs and we worked very hard to make ends meet. By now we had our three sons who needed our attention, and we had to take care of them. My husband worked one job and I worked one job. Eventually I had to work another job, so I ended up working two jobs and eventually three. I worked for a hotel in the day, and then I worked as a dining room manager at another hotel at night. Then when I got off of my shift I had to go and watch a lady who could not sleep all night. She had insomnia, and I had to stay awake to look after her. I would average about two hours of sleep a night. I had to depend on my husband and my neighbors to watch my children, as I thought that there was never enough money so I continued to work.

I missed my children growing up, and I became angry about that because as a mother, my dream was to see my children growing up, to go to Parent Teachers Association meetings, and to go to their sports events, and while I went to some, I missed out on so much more because I was working so hard.

Things got worse, and I cried out to my husband and begged him to bring about a change in our lives as I was so tired. At the time I looked up to him to remedy the financial crisis we had to endure.

We hit such tight spots that we did not even have food in the house at times. I remember always trying to keep Campbell's soup, crackers, and Kool-Aid in the house, because that is what I could afford under the circumstances. The lights, water, and telephone were constantly disconnected. Things were going from bad to worse. My husband handled the bills while I worked many hours. The thing that confused me the most was that I did not understand why they were not paid and why there were no groceries in the house. One day I was alerted by the mail that our home was $1,300.00 in the red and was in foreclosure. Our mortgage company said in the letter that if they knew they could find me that they knew I would fix it.

I drove to work very nervously, not knowing what to do. All I knew was that my life was taking a major turn in the wrong direction, and it was spinning out of control. The problem was that we were both making very good money weekly, so I did not understand why the bills weren't getting paid. I was praying at my desk in my office when I saw a Christian gentleman

I had not seen in years pass by my office. He must have noticed me, so he came back and stepped into my office and laid $1,300.00 on my desk and said, "I believe you might need this." I was so shocked that I asked him how he knew. He told me that God told him to give me the money. I immediately paid the house and got it current. I thanked God for what he had done; I was so grateful. But nothing let up as far as me working, so I continued to work even more. I even cleaned houses as well, so now I was working around the clock and nothing was getting any better. In fact things were getting a whole lot worse.

My children were suffering, and we did not even have money to buy them gifts for Christmas. All I could afford was Donald Duck shampoo and the little matchbox cars that I gave them for Christmas. Things continued to be very stressful. One day our phone was disconnected, and I got home and found that there was hardly any food in the house, so I prayed to God to have me find favor with a church or someone to help us with some groceries. In the past I had gone downtown in Indiana where they would help people in need. When I went into this building that I had never been in before, a gentleman met me and asked me what he could do for me. I told him that I needed food for my children. He asked me if I worked, as I was dressed as an office executive. I told him I did, and broke into tears, and he immediately sat me down and told me that he would take care of me with free food. He noticed that I was at the end of my rope. He did not know the story, but God used him to take care of us. You see I was so tired in my body, and the hours that I was working put a strain on me, therefore I was not aware of how the bills were being paid.

The Phone Call that Became a Blessing:

I left the house after I realized that we did not have food, and I had asked God for favor in the situation. I went to a pay phone as our phone was disconnected, and I still did not understand why, as I believed we made enough money to pay each bill that we incurred in our home. I searched through the yellow pages and found a church, so I called them. I believe God had let my eyes rest on that particular phone number at the time. A lady answered and said that they did not usually help anyone who does not go to their church. She placed me on hold for a second and then came back and asked me for my address, which I gave her. Within the hour this same lady showed up with big brown bags of groceries and put them on the kitchen table, went into the living room, and sat down.

In the meantime it was like Christmas for my boys, and they started unpacking those brown paper bags. They got so excited when they saw cereal, which we had not had in months. They shouted, "Mom we got cereal! Mom we got peanut putter. Mom there are steaks!" They had not seen food like this in a long time. I was so embarrassed that I told them to try to be quiet. I also had such good neighbors that I would call them and they would make sure they fed my children because they knew I was having such a hard time. This lady was sent from God to feed us with food for at least a month or two. May God bless her richly for what she did for our family.

I continued to work so hard that some days I felt so weak that I needed strength from the Lord to make it through the next day and the days thereafter. I wondered how long my body would hold up under the stress. By now my children were worried about me and told me that I needed to make a change in my life, or I was going to die. They were small at the time but very wise. I knew that they were right and that a change was inevitable.

The Christmas that Did Not Happen:

It was nearing Christmas and I dreaded it, as I knew that I did not have enough money to buy them presents again. As you know, a mother's dream is to buy her children presents for Christmas, which had not happened for me in many years. The wonderful thing about my three sons was that they were so patient. I sometimes think they thought that eventually things would change in their favor if they kept their attitude right in God's sight. We raised them to love the Lord, and I knew that's what got them through the hard times.

I received a call from my husband asking me to pickup a large bag of toys that his coworker gave him for us. I immediately got excited and went to his place of employment to pick it up. I knew that now I could wrap these toys and place them in the bay window so that when my children got up on Christmas day, they would be so excited. I wrapped these presents for about two hours and looked at the bay window and liked what I saw. We did not have a Christmas tree, so I had to do the best I could. I always believed that the financial stress was so unnecessary, but I realized I was not in control of the situation.

Christmas morning arrived and my three sons got up and were so excited to see the presents that they said, "Wow Mom!" We all sat on the floor and opened them when suddenly one of my sons cried out and said, "Mom these toys are broken." I could not believe that I wrapped toys that were broken in their boxes. They were mostly games, and I had no clue that this would happen. I had worked so many hours; I guess I should have checked each box, but from exhaustion I did not. I looked at them immediately and told them not to open another box. We pushed those boxes away, and I then told them to look into my eyes. While they were looking at their mom, I told them that this would be the last Christmas that they would not have anything, and I promised them that with the help of God, our very special visitor, I would change their lives as soon as I could.

Christmas day was a very sad time. They watched from the front door as they saw their friends with new bicycles and new toys. The thing that bothered me the most was that we had sufficient money for all our needs, but because of the many hours I worked, I was unable to oversee how the money was spent. The result was that my children did not enjoy a good Christmas once again, and eventually my marriage ended. I will continue to say that throughout the hard times, I am thankful to the Lord for blessing me with three very special sons, whom I love with all my heart.

Chapter 13

THE CHANGE THAT HAPPENED ON NEW YEAR'S EVE NIGHT

J was alone on New Year's Eve as my children were with my ex-husband. I was very sad and felt rather blue, but somehow I was very optimistic that the Lord had greater plans for my life, which I was not totally aware of. While I was pondering about my life and wondering why it had taken such a turn, I was startled to hear a knock on my front door. I opened it, and to my amazement I saw one of my best friends, Gail, standing in front of me. I invited her in and told her that it was a surprise to see her. She told me that she wanted to take me out to church to see the New Year in and that she also wanted me to meet someone very special. I told her

I just wanted to stay home and that I did not want to see anyone that evening. She was very persistent and continued to pursue what she came for.

After a long time I finally agreed, so I got dressed and went with her to this church in Louisville, Kentucky. While we were in the lobby she drew my attention to a gentleman who was standing and talking to other people at the time. I was totally shocked at who it was because I had been to the church where he was associate pastor about three times, and I noticed he had a major anointing on his life and that he was a fantastic musician who played a mean grand piano. He had an outstanding voice, and I had seen him playing with the faith quartet at one of the services I was invited to. In fact after my divorce I was invited with my three sons to go to a Sunday morning service by a wonderful friend of the family. We all ran to the altar and got on our knees and asked God to change our lives that morning, which He did. I then was invited again, and this time I sat in the back because I got there late due to working my regular three jobs. During the service I again noticed that this associate pastor was very anointed, and I was sure he was married so I proceeded to ask the Lord that when he redid my life, if he would give me someone just like him.

Gail fulfilled her mission and introduced me to John House, the associate pastor of Christ Assembly in Louisville, Kentucky. I was blown away, because all the thoughts of what I had asked God for came back, except now they were becoming a reality. He sat next to me in church that evening, and by the end of the service the pastor asked us to stand up and join hands. He continued to say that whoever you were holding hands with was more than likely the person you would be with the following year. Little did I know that New Year's Eve night would bring about a new change in my life.

After church was over I walked towards Gail's car, as she had brought me to church that night. She told me that there was no room in her car and that I had to go with John in his truck, as he had more room. I did not understand why she suddenly would not let me in her car, but then I realized she had all this planned with John and they had worked together for this blind date on New Year's Eve. I proceeded to get into his truck, and he drove me home while Gail and her family came over to my home as well. We watched Christian television while we talked. Eventually it was getting late, so Gail and her family left. John stayed a little while longer and left an hour later to go home. Before he left he asked me for my telephone number, which I did not want to give him. I was raised so straight laced that I was always told that a lady does not give out her telephone number. I finally did so he could contact me.

The next morning he called me and asked me if he could take me to a restaurant in Indiana for breakfast and if he could look at my car, which I was having trouble with at the time. I told him that was all right and that I would go with him that morning. Everything changed after that as he took me and my boys out to restaurants. He fed them to make sure they had enough to eat. He started bringing dishes, blankets, and sheets over, as I was low on everything. In other words, he took us under his wing and continued to make sure we were taken care of. He eventually gave my sons their first Christmas tree with presents around it, and we knew that God had sent him into our lives. We were so thankful to have someone care about us again and that maybe some of the suffering was finally over. God never promised us a rose garden; He promised to walk with us through all the tough times.

I remember one Christmas my eldest son told John a story about how I was working very late one evening. It was a very cold winter's night, and they had called my place of work to ask me if I could go to a Mexican restaurant in Indiana, which was on the way home, and bring them some tacos and burritos. I continued to tell them that I only had $7.00 on me and that I had to have gas to get back to work the next day, but that I would do the best I could to bring the food home for them. I proceeded to count my money with all the change and found out that I could only afford three burritos, which I took home that evening. I sat down with them at the table and placed one burrito onto each of their plates. They asked me what I was going to eat, and I told them that I was fine and that I was going to eat a lettuce sandwich, as I had lettuce in the fridge. Sometimes I could eat at work but not always because I was so busy. So of course I was hungry also, but I did not let them know this.

They cut their burritos in half and put them on another plate so that I could eat as well. I have repeatedly told you how good my children were; this time they brought me to tears. I placed the half burritos back onto their plates, as they needed to eat to retain their strength. I always gave them lunch money so they could eat at school. Eventually things got so bad that they used to get free lunches. After they told this story to John, I could see that he was not going to let my boys suffer anymore but was going to look after them from then on, which made me feel so relieved and so grateful to the Lord for bringing him to us.

John and I started dating and going to Christ Assembly, where he was associate pastor. My boys used to love to watch him play the piano. They loved to watch him move his feet while he kept the rhythm and run his hands over the keyboard. I felt that he was one of the best piano players in Louisville, Kentucky. Since he was blessed with the wonderful voice that God gave him, we both sang together many times for the Lord.

We eventually got married at Christ Assembly in Louisville and embarked on a journey with six children between us. John had two girls and a boy from a previous marriage, and I had three boys from my previous marriage. I enjoyed all his children so much and I loved them as my own, and he loved my boys as his own. I had his children on weekends and enjoyed cooking their favorite foods for them every time they came over. We both loved the Lord with all our hearts and wanted nothing other than the direction of the Holy Spirit in our lives and in our futures as well. If I told you it was easy, that would be a lie. It was not always, but John and I kept the faith, and we always put God first in our lives. We prayed together, studied the Word together, and always enjoyed God talking to us about our very next move. In fact it became exciting as we listened to the voice of God to direct us on our new journey.

Chapter 14

HEARING FROM HEAVEN

*O*ne night after we came home from church, I was reading my Bible and the Lord told me that I had to leave Indiana and go to Florida. I shared this with John, and he said, "If God is in it, we need to go." I felt it so strongly the next morning that before I went to work, I told him to have a yard sale and that if he got a certain amount of money, we would leave for Florida in the next few days. He called me that afternoon and told me that he had just received the amount that we needed. I knew we were embarking on a new stage of our lives that we knew nothing about. When you hear from heaven, it makes all the difference in the world.

We packed my children up in one of the cars we had and set out for Florida. In the meantime I had sold my good-looking Cadillac and given John's ex-wife the money for child support so that he would not get behind while looking for a job in Florida. The children were not happy to leave their friends and their basketball. My sons were very good basketball players and had received numerous trophies for their winnings. I tried to explain to them that this would be the best move and that it could change their lives forever.

We placed a case of oil on the back floorboard, as the car we were taking to Florida had a major oil leak. John and I had both been through so much, but somehow we knew the car would get us safely to Florida. We left Indiana and set out for Florida. After driving many, many hours we saw the palm trees glistening in the night, and we realized we were getting close to our destination.

John had driven most of the way, so I took my turn at driving into Tampa while he slept for a while. Unfortunately the lights went out totally in our car, and a semi truck driver in front of me put his lights on bright and stayed in front of me, as I believe he saw I had a problem. I drove in his light all the way into Tampa, Florida. When we got to Tampa in the early hours of the morning, we rested a while from our journey. We made sure we had eaten enough and then we started out for Sarasota, which was about an hour or so away. We were headed for my brother's house in Sarasota where we were going to stay and help him, as he had injured his back.

We got to our destination safely, and it was good to see my brother again. After a good night's sleep, we awoke the next morning, and my very special visitor prompted me to go and apply for a position at the convenience store. It was a few blocks down the road, within walking distance. The Holy Spirit told me that I would get hired immediately. I applied and I was hired right away. This taught me that God never makes mistakes. I now had a job, and John had a temporary job with my brother. He worked for a while in drywall and then later took a position at a restaurant chain.

He walked into the restaurant one morning and asked if they had any openings. He was in a black suit, white shirt, and a tie, which he was used to wearing, as he was a minister. The only thing is that John was not aware of how casually the Floridians dressed, so the manager immediately told him that he had one opening but that he was too classy for the position. John continued to tell him that he had just married a lady with three little boys and had to make sure they were taken care of. John told the manager that he would sweep the floors and do whatever it took to bring in money for his family. This was very commendable, as looking for the job he was used to would take time, and he needed money right away.

Eventually the manager told him that he had a dishwasher position available. John proceeded to tell him that he would accept it. He worked as a dishwasher for two months or so, and I worked as a waitress on the graveyard shift, while also working at the convenience store. While at the convenience store, I was promoted to assistant manager and then I referred John, so he worked with me at the same store. We now had two jobs apiece. One thing I knew was that we were both hard-working people.

As we continued to work so hard, we were offered even better positions, which we accepted to accomplish our goals and to get us on our feet financially. We put our three boys through school and made sure that they achieved their goals as well. They enjoyed sports, so they immediately went right into basketball, which they had so enjoyed while in Indiana. Today two of them are coaches for basketball teams in Florida, and mom is very proud of their achievements.

Chapter 15

THE MOVE TO FLORIDA THAT CHANGED OUT LIVES FOREVER

*W*e continued to work very hard when one day a customer entered my place of employment and offered me a job I could not refuse. She was the manager of a large retail store in Sarasota, Florida. I told her I would go for the interview but that I was very nervous because I had not worked in a department store before.

I had worked previously in Louisville, Kentucky in the food business, which was my expertise. I worked for Rodeway Inn as banquet coordinator and dining room manager. I also worked for the Holiday Inn and Louisville Inn. One of the largest catering companies in New Albany, Indiana offered me a position as the personnel director of over 300 people. The owner did catering on a very large scale, and I was put in charge of the semi-trucks, box trucks, menus, and other organizational duties. One day I asked my manager if I could hire my husband as my fleet manager, which he allowed, as this was beyond my job description and I needed help. I had enough to do in the personnel department. We catered the Arabian horse shows in Lexington, Kentucky and the Kentucky Ham Breakfast for the State Fair in Louisville. I also organized the Bob Hope special in the Civic Center. I did the floor plans and scheduled the personnel for that event. You may think, "Why did you leave Indiana?" It was because God had called us to Florida, and we had to obey.

I had continued to learn all I could in retail in Florida so that I could grow with this company, when one day another large retailer bought us out, and we had to find other employment.

One night I had a spiritual dream, where all the employees walked on a wide road towards finding positions elsewhere. I alone found myself on a narrow road. I had to go through a rocky path until I came to this huge store, and a lady opened up the door to me. She said, "Whatever is in this building is yours." There was fruit everywhere, which spoke of the fruitfulness I could expect on my journey. While my friends all went to the outlet mall close by, I was the only one who went to one of the largest retail stores in Florida. This store saw my potential and made me a manager in a very short time. They even flew me to Miami, where I gave a speech to approximately 250 people on the topic of "What Makes Me Successful." There was a big round of applause, which expressed to me that they enjoyed it immensely. The president and the board congratulated me, and they presented me with a large golden eagle statue. The reason for the eagle was very special to me. I always taught my employees not to be ducks but to be eagles. I believe eagles never lose their focus, and they do not flock; you find them one at a time.

I continued to grow with this company and became very successful. It was at the peak of my success when God moved us in a different direction one more time. We were obedient to the change he wanted for us, as we had felt deep inside our hearts for many years that we would start our own company. This meant that we would be financially independent, which we welcomed at the time.

Things became very clear as God opened up many doors that created a major change in our life.

Chapter 16

ANGEL VISITATION

One day I decided to sit on my patio and enjoy the sunshine while the ducks were swimming on the lake. Everything was so beautiful and peaceful. The blue jays were flying around, and the little squirrels were running up and down the trees. I thought to myself one more time that the creator was again in charge of this day. I felt so calm, and I decided to bring a notebook and a pen so that I could write my thoughts on paper if need be. Suddenly I felt like there was someone standing right beside me, and I felt a presence I could not explain. I sat quietly in reverence when I was prompted by the Holy Spirit to write about our company we were starting in Florida. The words flowed so eloquently, and things that I could not imagine were written by the prophetic hand of God. I believe that there was an angel standing next to me during every page I wrote. You see he told us about starting our company AYS, Inc.—which stands for At Your Service. The Lord told me that he had given His angels direction to be at our service to make our business grow in Bradenton. He told me that our business would prosper and that it would be a most unusual angelic business, as it would meet the needs of many a hurting soul. It has done just that. We prayed and studied the Word of God often so that we would not miss what God wanted to do with our business in Florida. He told me that the name AYS stood for the following—All Year Seed. God told us that once we no longer worked for an employer and stepped out in faith, there would not be a day without income in our business, as He would be sure that we always had all year seed.

It was not unusual for us to see angels appear in our home and to have the Lord tell us what our next move was for our company. We obeyed and listened and wrote down everything that God told us, and we cherished it daily. We started our business in September 1996, and it has become an amazing business and a mission field for every hurting soul along the way. Until now everything that God told us has come to pass. We now own AYS, Inc., which is a limousine service in Bradenton, Florida. We are thankful to the Lord for the many blessings He has bestowed upon us. I am reminded of the scripture in Matthew 9:23, "Jesus said unto him, if thou canst believe, all things are possible to him that believeth." We believe everything God tells us in His Word because we have learnt over the years in our spiritual journey that through Him, all things become possible.

After we started our business and as we pursued God's presence, angel visitation increased. One evening I went to bed feeling sick with a sinus infection. I developed a sinus infection for about two years, and my face became very sore and swollen, and I had to have medication from the doctor. Somehow I knew that God could heal me as He had done so many times before, so I put on worship music that infiltrated our bedroom and set the stage for my healing. After a while I turned the music off and went to sleep.

In the early hours of the morning, I was awakened by music and the ringing of bells. I looked in amazement as an angel with the prettiest shiny golden hair stood over my bed in white attire.

Above me I saw a huge wheel in the ceiling, spinning with a smaller wheel inside of it. I saw angels flying around the room, something I had not experienced before. The angel smiled and looked right at me, standing very still. While he stood still, something was happening to my face. The best way I can describe it was that it felt like a vacuum was placed on my face to release the pressure I was feeling. I raised my hand and praised the Lord loudly and woke my husband up. He asked me if I was all right. I said that I was but that he would never believe me if I told him that I was awakened by an angel. I lay very still in my bed, in awe after the encounter and could not move for a while. When I eventually got the energy to get off my bed to go to the restroom, I was electrified all over my body, as I could not see the angel but felt he had not left the room. When I finally got back into bed, I felt the presence of the angel again. I lay still and quiet, thinking over the Godly encounter I had just seen with my own eyes. I asked God to let me know what this all meant. He does not tell us everything at the time, but I was given the following words, "You will see things you have never seen; you will hear things you have never heard; you will do things you've never done, and you will go places you have never been."

One of the things I have never done is write a book, so I believe this is part of the Word of the Lord that I received during this time. The following morning I awoke with tenderness in my face, and my husband said that he noticed I no longer had nasal drip from the sinuses. We both got excited and realized that the vacuuming I felt was when the angel cleaned out my sinuses. I believe that was in 1996, and I have not had any sinus trouble since. In fact when the dentist checked me, he made the comment on what clean sinus cavities I had. When I told him and the nurse what happened, they could not believe it, but nevertheless it was a testimony to them of God's miracle-working power.

Shortly after we started our business, I began taking a born-again businesswoman to Tampa. She was very hungry for the Lord and needed to learn more about God's Word. I invited her and her husband to Bible study, so they started to come weekly. We had a great time when they came over, and I was amazed at how much they soaked up the Word of God.

One evening while driving her home, she said she had something to tell me. She proceeded to tell me about an incident in another city where she used to live. She said she had an accident and had hurt her nose. The pain was so bad that she prayed to the Lord, and suddenly an angel walked in and told her that she would meet someone named Gloria who would teach her the Word of God. I immediately told her that I had seen this angel in our home often and described the attire that he wore. She told me that was exactly what he had on. We both got excited and knew right then and there that God had brought about a divine appointment for her and I to meet. The Lord is so awesome.

I have always believed that we need to create an environment for the Holy Spirit to dwell in. When you worship the Lord, He moves in and I believe that ultimate worship is the key to accessing the glory from the throne room of heaven. One cannot even understand the depths and heights that God can take you to when you worship. He will open the windows of heaven upon your life and release blessings that you cannot contain.

You have to welcome Him into your days and nights. I know that we have to occupy until He comes, but we still have to find time to spend with our creator.

I am reminded of a word the Lord gave to me on July 27, 1997.

I want this home to be a vessel, clean and pure and fit for the Master's use. In order for me to bless you abundantly, you have to welcome me into your days and into your nights. Remember I made these days, and I made those nights because I want to talk to you. Occupy until I come but please spend quality time on a daily basis so I can alert you of the pitfalls that Satan will try to bring across your path because of the mighty anointing that I have placed in this home. The more time you spend with me, the Holy Spirit, the sooner I open each window of my glory. I just speak, and each window opens and you can take out of that window what you want, because I am giving it to you because you are my inheritance. I wish I could really make you understand what I am doing in your midst. It is truly astronomical. There are conditions, however. You must pray without ceasing. Spend time in the Word and fast. If you do all these things, the glory is going to burst forth so strong that you will not be able to contain it. I will then release the final window of my glory over this home, and you will reach the ultimate plan and my anointing before my coming. AYS will also be very significant in these last days as a means of transport, to bring about security and comfort to those who feel insecure. I am just getting you ready for a mighty move, so prepare yourselves and stay blameless while I guide and teach you on a daily basis.

We listened to His voice daily and still do because not hearing His voice in every decision we make can be detrimental to our lives. With the help of God, we can become good listeners.

Chapter 17

THE GIFT FROM MY CREATOR

After the Lord healed me, I started listening to His voice even more. I did not want to miss what He had to tell me, so daily it became very exciting to hear His voice, and as I did it changed my life. I became very aware of His ongoing guidance and enjoyed it when He directed my paths. Proverbs 3:6 says, "In all thy ways acknowledge Him, and He will direct your paths."

I was given very specific instructions concerning a trip that I was going to take to South Africa in 1998. The Lord told me that I would not leave on the date that I had arranged, but that He had a different plan and time for my departure to my homeland. I had not seen my family for a very long time and was missing them all.

The Gentleman I Met on a Plane:

When I was having my quiet time with the Lord on March 17, 1998 I received the following message from the Lord.

> This is a new garden of my presence. Bask in it and I will let you smell my glory. Walk through in faith, and I will surprise you with all the answers.
>
> You will leave and have a safe trip. You will witness to a very specific person that I have placed on your flight. The reason you have not left yet is because this person is not flying until your documents are processed. It is imperative that you touch the heart of this person, which is why you have not left earlier. This person is a gentleman of renown, and only your anointing and gifts that I have placed upon you since a child will be able to touch his heart at my direction. Do not think this strange; it is not. This man needs me, and

this is his very last chance to know me. You will penetrate his soul. This is why you will be leaving at a very specific time. You will be much anointed with my presence on the plane and when you get home to see your family. So do not fear anymore; this is in my hands. Take it a day at a time, and once again once your documents leave Florida, an angel will carry them specifically to the correct source where they will be processed expediently and be sent right back to you. By this time your ticket will be purchased very easily. Stay under my leadership, and I will show you the inevitable. Do not worry anymore about the timing and the hardships concerning all of your paperwork and the runaround you have received, it was all in my plan. There is a very special time for you to leave; this man needs help and you have been ordained before the foundation of the world to reach him. Trust, trust, and do not get impatient. Your trip is very special, very specific, and ordained by Me.

This message came to pass on the way home from South Africa to Florida. On the return trip I sat by the window, and there were two empty seats next to me. It was a night flight, so I made myself comfortable and waited for the gentleman the Lord told me was about to show up.

After a while a man sat in the same row as me, leaving a seat open between us. I wondered if it was he. He began ordering all kinds of liquor, and it was as though he was trying to deaden his feelings. He looked rather unhappy, so I could not wait to talk to him, but I wanted God to open up the conversation. I asked the Lord if this was the man, and I heard a very distinct voice in my spirit say, "That's him."

So around two in the morning I finally opened the conversation, and he talked and talked all night long. He had lost most of his family in 1996 when the Pan American flight went down, so he had a lot of questions, which I tried to help him with. He had been working in Cape Town as a professor but lived in America. I tried, with the help of the Lord, to instill in his heart that he needed to build a relationship with the Holy Spirit. I believed he listened to me and felt the urgency in my voice as I said the following words, "I was put on this plane just for you." He told me that he was on the same plane as me traveling from America to South Africa, but that he did not sit next to me at the time. He could not believe that God would single him out and place someone next to him to help him with his life.

We communicated after he came back to the United States, and suddenly I received a call from him that his wife had left him. He let me pray for him on the phone and then I never heard from him again. I am so glad that I obeyed the Lord during this time. Thank you Jesus for Your guidance. I learned a lot from the Holy Spirit as my prophetic gift continued to grow

The Miracle that Happened to My Sister Judith on June 29, 2005:

My sister Judy, her husband, and her wonderful family live in Cape Town, South Africa.

Her husband was her soul mate and they loved each other so much. They began dating in their school days and finally married and had three beautiful children. Her husband became ill, and one day he died very suddenly. This was too much for her to bear, so she grieved for a very long time. I flew home shortly after that to spend time with her. She could not understand why God took her husband home. I tried to help her with all her questions and spent some quality time with her.

After I got back to Florida, I received a phone call from my mom concerning my sister Judy. Her voice was full of urgency.

She continued to tell me that Judy was just rushed to the hospital hemorrhaging, and that the doctors did not know what was wrong with her. The Lord immediately told me to tell my mom to tell the doctor right away that Judy had a stomach aneurism. I spoke to Judy in the hospital and told her that God would bring her through this, as I had prayed for her, and I believe in God answering our prayers. The doctor checked and found a stomach bleed. Right after that Judy developed a brain aneurism as well, so she went into surgery right away. They stopped the bleed in the brain, but she was still in critical condition.

I received another phone call from mom telling me that she made it through the surgery but that I needed to pray because they were rushing her back into surgery again, as this was much more serious. She had a blood clot in her brain and might not make it. I prayed with my mom and told her that God was going to raise up a certain doctor who knew what to do for her, and that is exactly what happened. She had major surgery, as they had to cut her skull open to remove the blood clot. It was touch and go, but still I communicated to my family that God was not done with Judy and that she would not die but would live to declare the wondrous works of the Lord.

While I was traveling to Tampa, Florida, I was prompted by the Holy Spirit to pull off the road and go to the rest stop so He could talk to me about Judy. I obeyed. I always keep a notebook close at all times incase the Lord tells me some important things that I need to document, so after I pulled into the rest stop, I began praying to the Lord and asked Him what his plan was for my sister.

I received the following message at 12:55p.m. on June 29, 2005:

I have heard your prayers. I have heard your cries all my children, Judy shall not die but live to declare the wondrous works of the Lord. This will catapult her into a new relationship with me, saith the Lord. I will take her to a new level in a spiritual walk, saith the God of Abraham, Isaac and Jacob. She will grow in me and experience rivers of my glory as she becomes obedient to my voice. I will take her from one river to another, where she will experience inner peace and joy that she has not felt for some time.

Through all the heartache and suffering, I have never left her and will continue to stay by her side. All she has to do is listen to my voice and stay very focused on me in the next two weeks. There is no time in this world you're living in but to serve me in spirit and in truth. Judy, I have you in the palm of my hand. Do not forget that I love you and will comfort you always. Take care of your family spiritually, and you will see them also receive a new vision of me as never before. Your sickness has caused a change in the hearts of many, and what the devil meant for bad in your life, I turned it for good. Judy, you will not die but live. I will heal your body, saith your God. Trust me now, and I will show you my glory and my power will stay with you as long as you love me.

Do not worry about anything. Each issue in your life, whether it be family or any other problem, I will go through each one of them with you one miracle at a time. Judy, remember

I died for you and blessed you many years with a wonderful husband, children, and life. Count your blessings and remember the good times I let you experience in those years. However it is now time to focus on the future and watch out for you and your family. It is my will for all of you to be very close to me in these last days. I am coming back, so prepare yourself, saith your God. Live a life holy and acceptable to me. You are my child, Judy, and again I say you will not die but live to declare the wondrous works of the Lord.

In Psalms 118: 17, the Word of God says the following: "I shall not die, but live, and declare the works of the Lord."

Judy came through the second surgery but could not talk and was in a coma. She was unresponsive, so the doctor told my family to go home and rest and to wait and see what would happen. He told us she might come through it, but the chances were slim. My mom and I prayed again on the phone, and I assured her that the Word from the Lord mentioned the next two weeks, and I continued to tell mom that she would wake up on the fourteenth day. I told her to go home and not to worry because God had it all in control.

On the fourteenth day, one of my sisters came to see Judy, and the nurse suggested she wake her up. She replied that "She does not wake up." She woke Judy up, and she sat up in bed and asked for chocolate chip cookies and apple juice. She also asked if anyone had remembered mom's birthday and if they had bought a present for her. Her mind was totally alert, praise be to the Lord. We thank Him for healing Judy. What an awesome God we serve.

Chapter 18

RELEASE THEM TO FLY

*G*od continued to lead me to many a person, even on the street, that I could help in their time of need.

Each time I would talk to someone it would be a divine appointment, and God always became the center of it all. The Lord is so good. He sends us to so many hurting souls who have dreams like we do but that are yet unfulfilled.

RELEASE THEM TO FLY, written by Gloria House on February 12, 2004

Do not think it strange when each day you meet
a person I have sent you on the street.

I have sent them for a purpose, that sometimes you may
never know
but yet to you I've sent them with all their hurts
and woes,
You have never known why sometimes you've met these
people dear,
but I tell you child, it is my plan while you are still
down here.
You have cheered many I have sent your way, prayed
with many a soul
each day, yet I know you often wonder,
Lord what is your plan for these dear ones as you ponder.

Yes daughter, there is a plan that you are learning
each day.
And that is to show these souls I am sending your way,
the life and hope that they can find in only Jesus'name.
Yes this is an amazing time I say,
when my plan is placed your way,
because many, many more times there will be,
when I will send you total strangers you see.
People from all walks of life that I have sent you from
my sight,
I have dispatched them to you dear, for you to teach
them not to fear.
After you have done what I called you to do, release
them to fly.

Yes fly they must, and with my help they will soar over
mountains high,
Over many trials and temptations until they reach
the sky.
My plan for them made clear by now by you, my child,
whom I chose to use in these last days,
will be fulfilled in many of them as they take wings
and fly.
Release them to fly, my daughter, release them to fly,
through many trials, hurts, and ills, they will however come
They will come through, I say, they will come through,
because as they spread their wings to fly,
I will accompany them and together we will fly so high.

Daughter thank you for your obedience to me to
everyone you meet.
Continue to expand my Word to everyone on the street.
Relentless you are, when each soul you see needs me
throughout their daily journey.
Yes relentless you are, when they are hurting so,
Time is no issue to you at this point, because they
need me so.

All you see is someone who needs to be taken out of the
devil's hands
and placed within my outstretched, everlasting arms.

After this process has taken place one more time,
Release them child to fly; fly they must and fly they will,
Into my presence quiet and still.
In my presence is the fullness of joy without measure,
show them my ways daily, teach them to treasure the
Lord their God
and together we will all fly to higher heights before my
returning,
which could be anytime when I call home my bride.
Fly child, fly and together we will release them to fly.

The Lord has remarkably prepared every avenue of my life for every divine appointment that I have encountered with the many people He has sent to me. I am so honored to be this great part of His plan in these troublesome times.

My prayer for you is that He will make every unfulfilled dream in your life a reality.

May the Lord lift up His countenance upon you and give you peace. (Numbers 6:26)

CPSIA information can be obtained
at www.ICGtesting.com
Printed in the USA
BVHW042024120620
581231BV00006B/222

9 781498 451451